Halloween's time
Color for relax

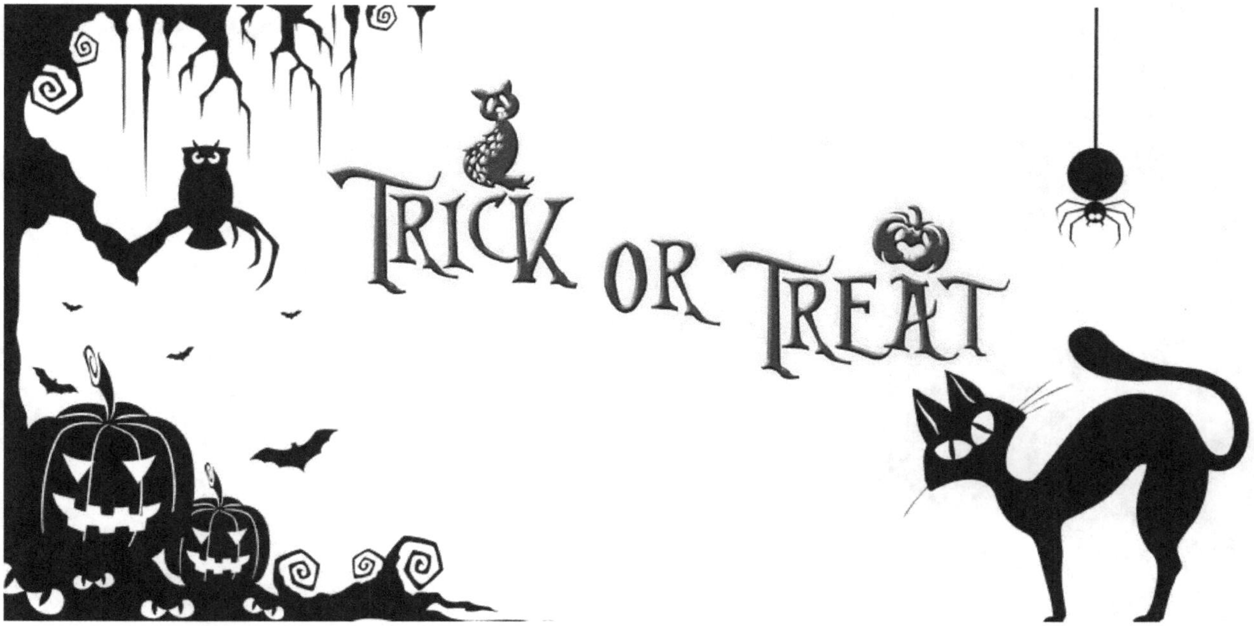

Honey M. Brown

Halloween's time
Color for relax

Copyright: Published in the United States by Honey M. Brown
Published October 2016

ISBN-13: 978-1539815440
ISBN-10: 1539815447

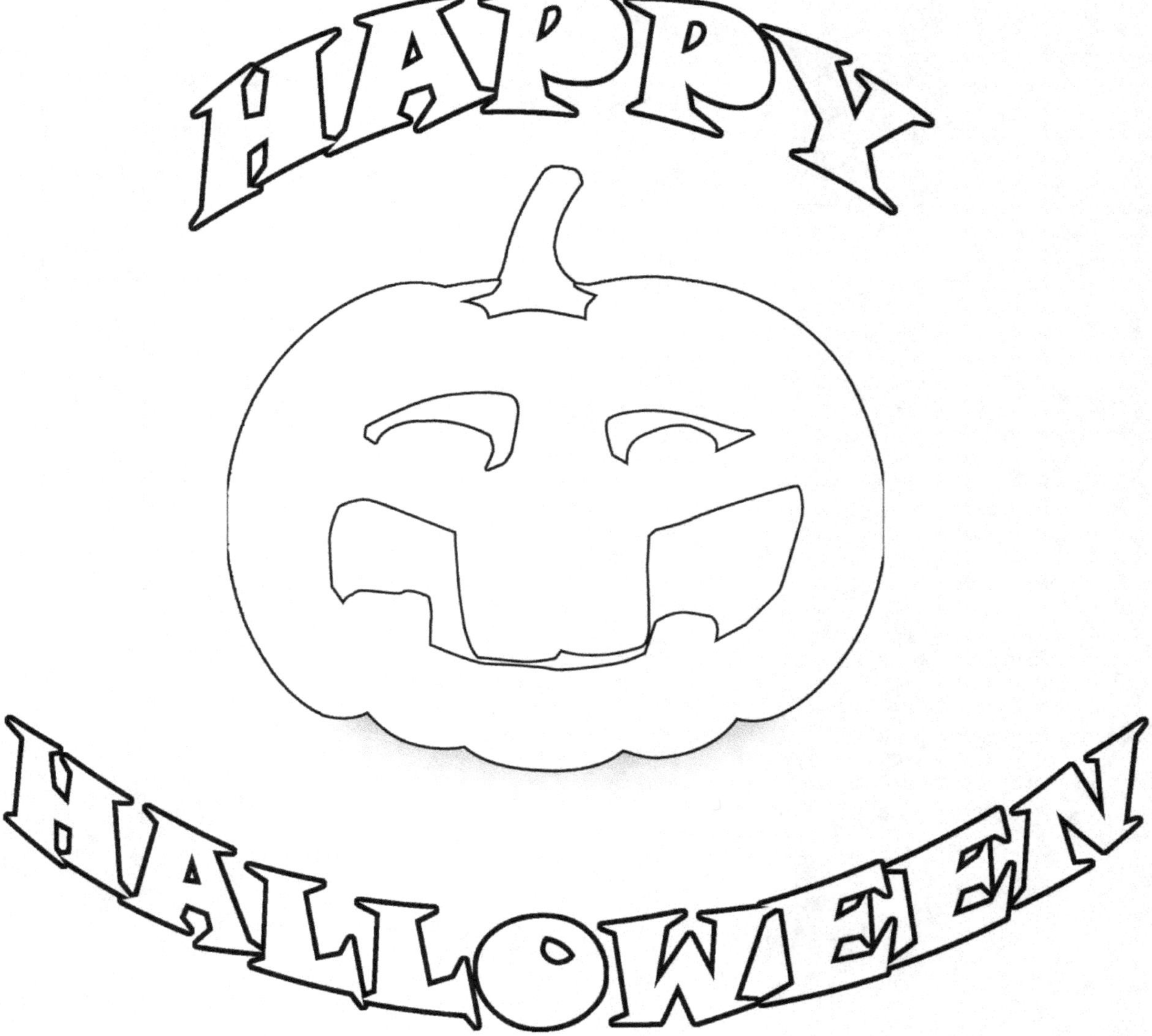
HAPPY
HALLOWEEN

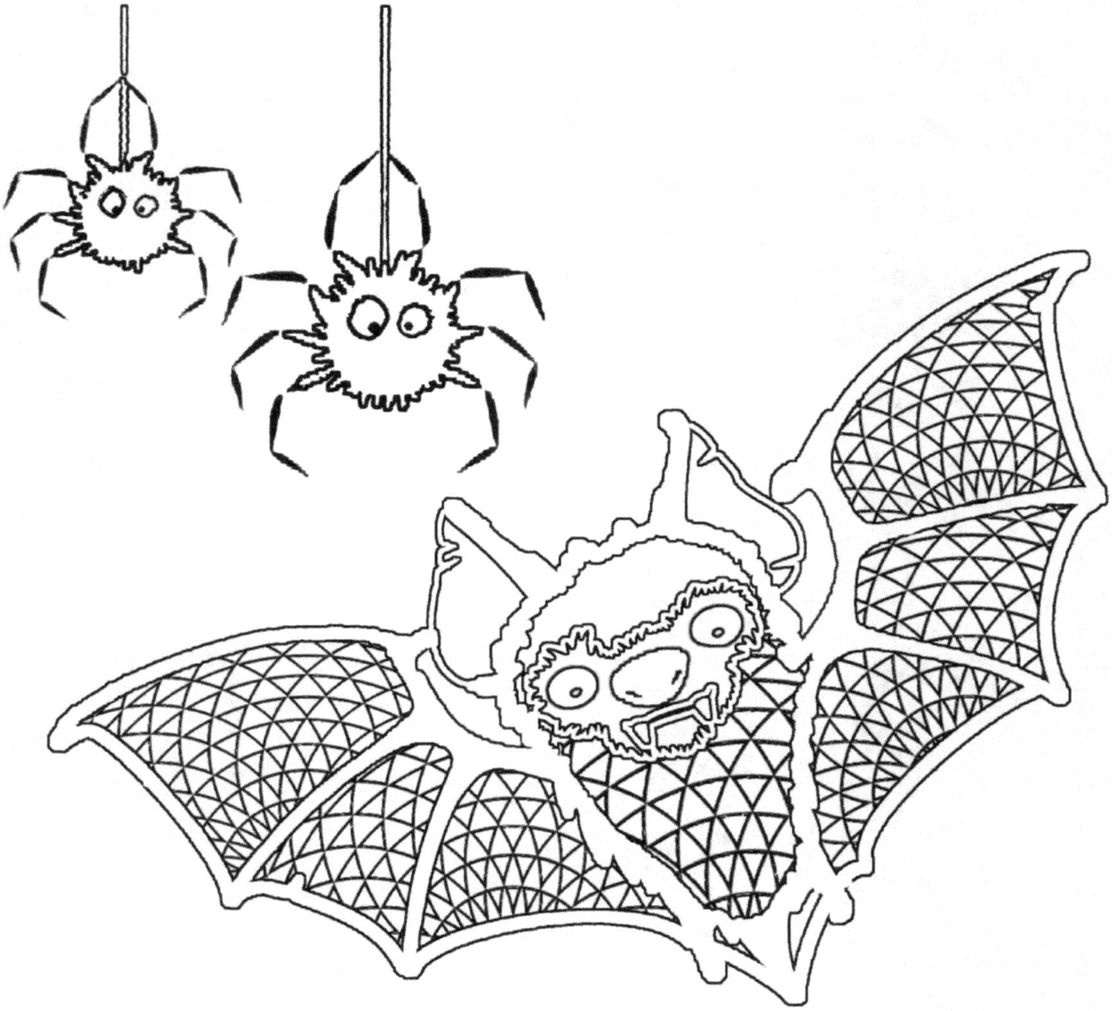

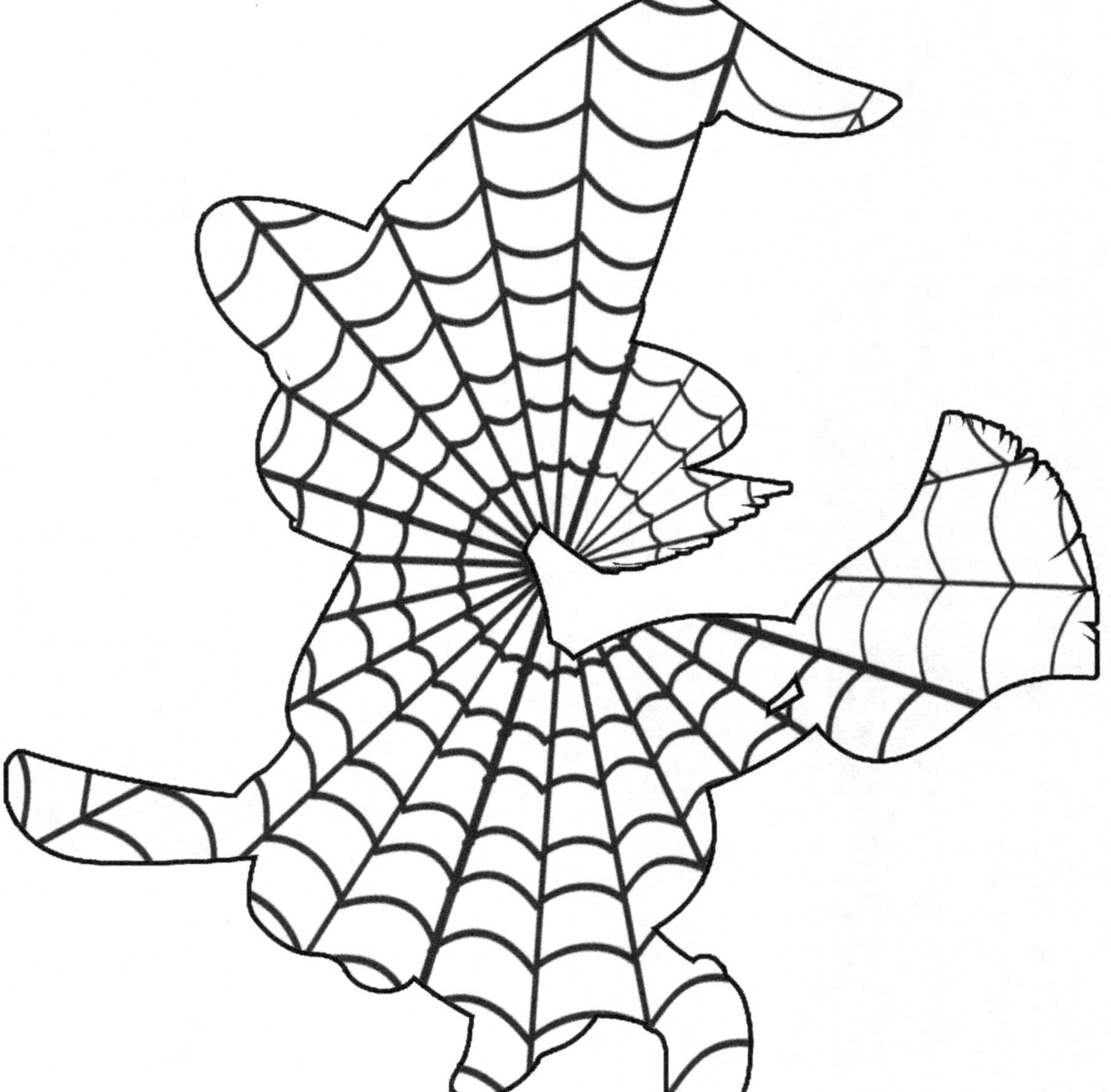

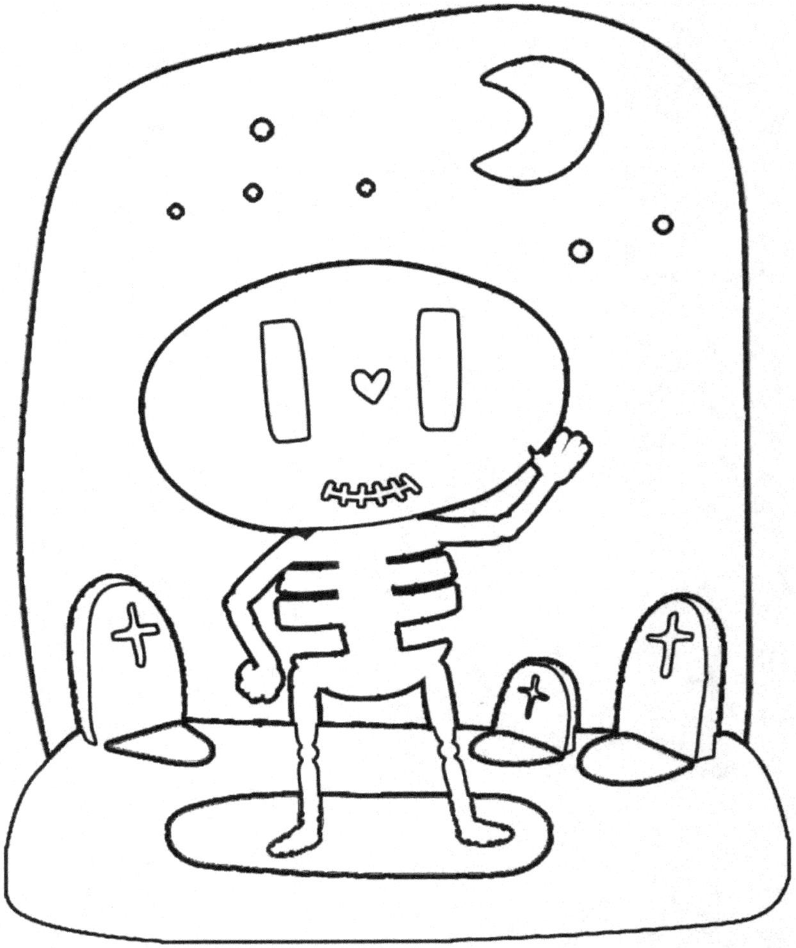

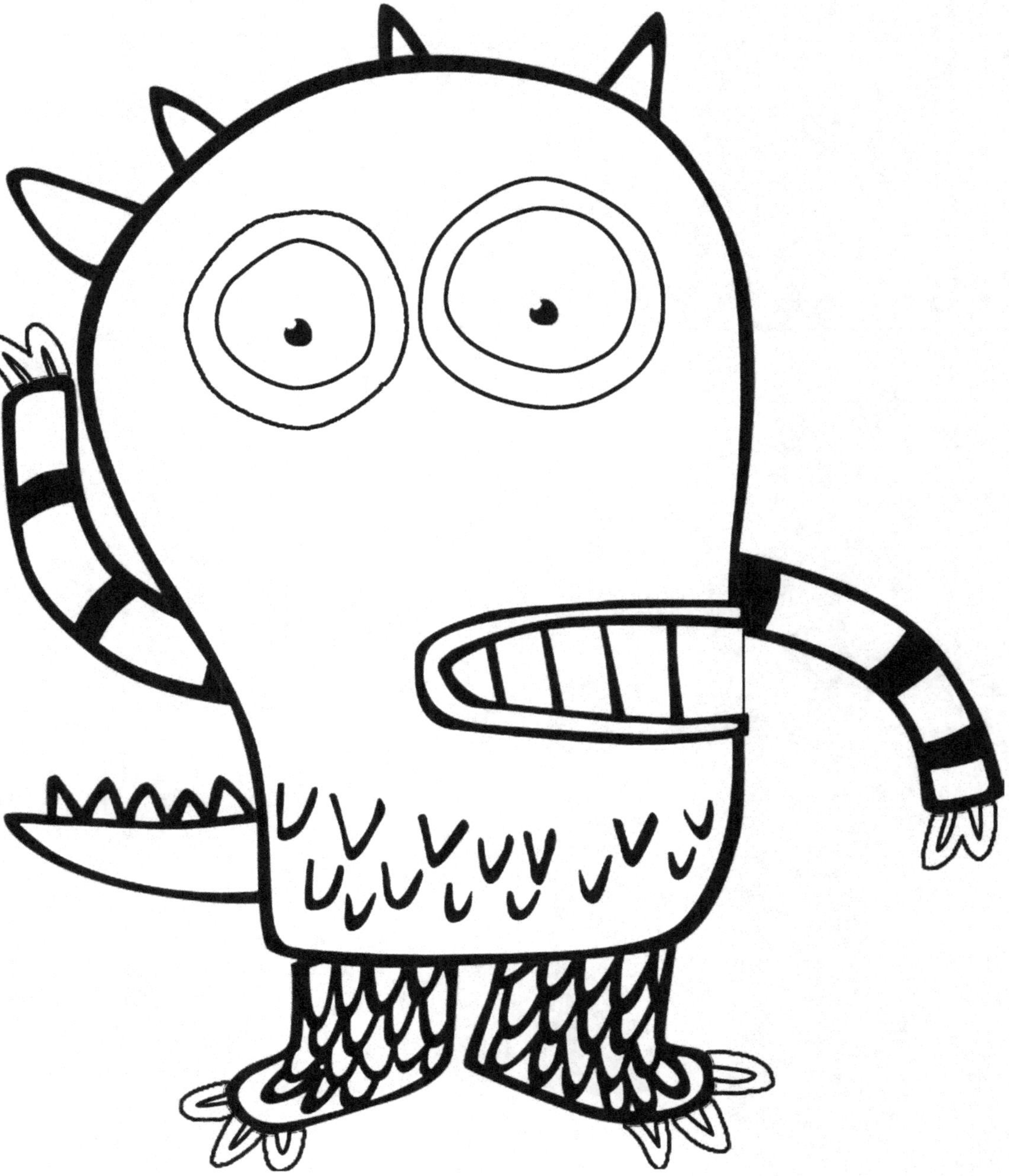

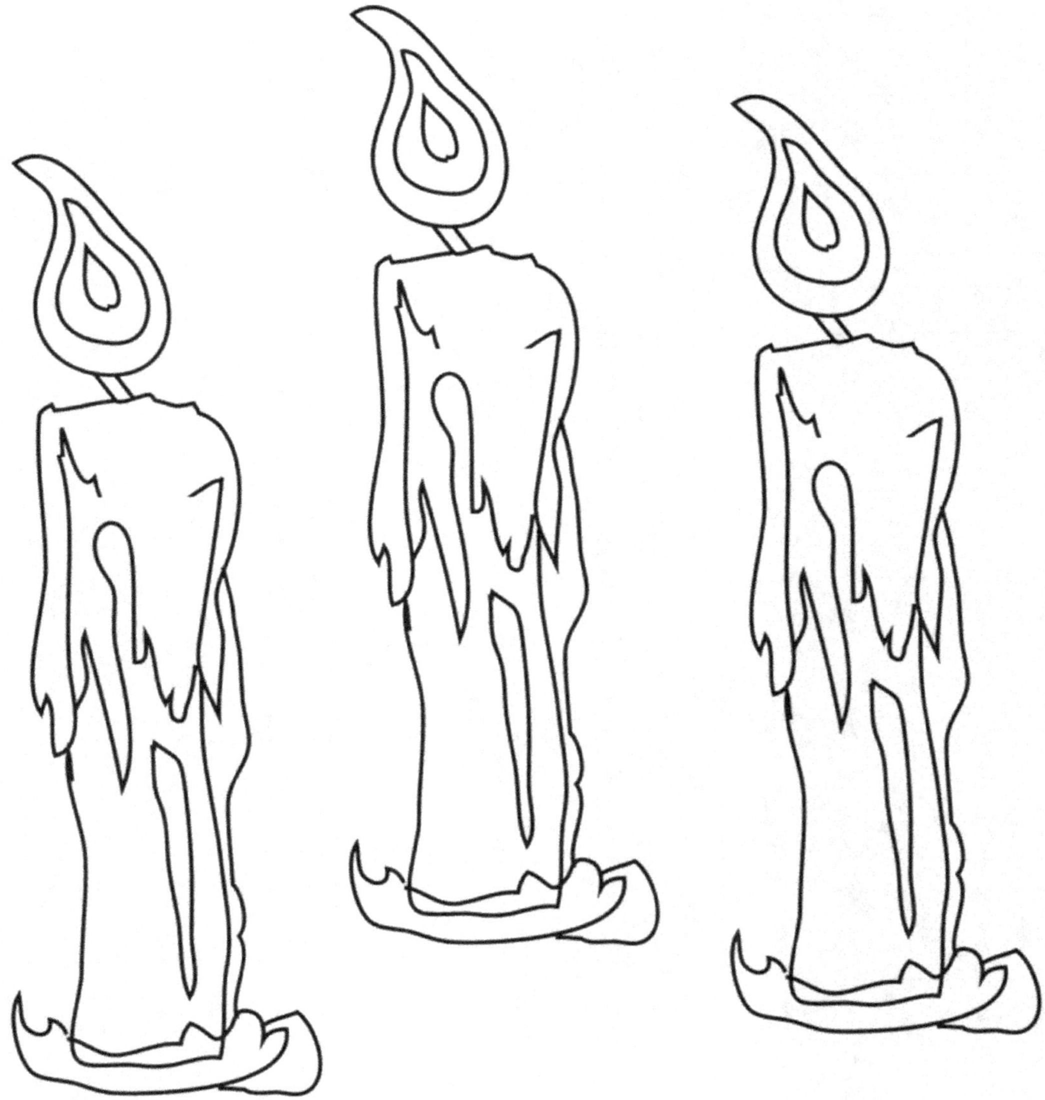

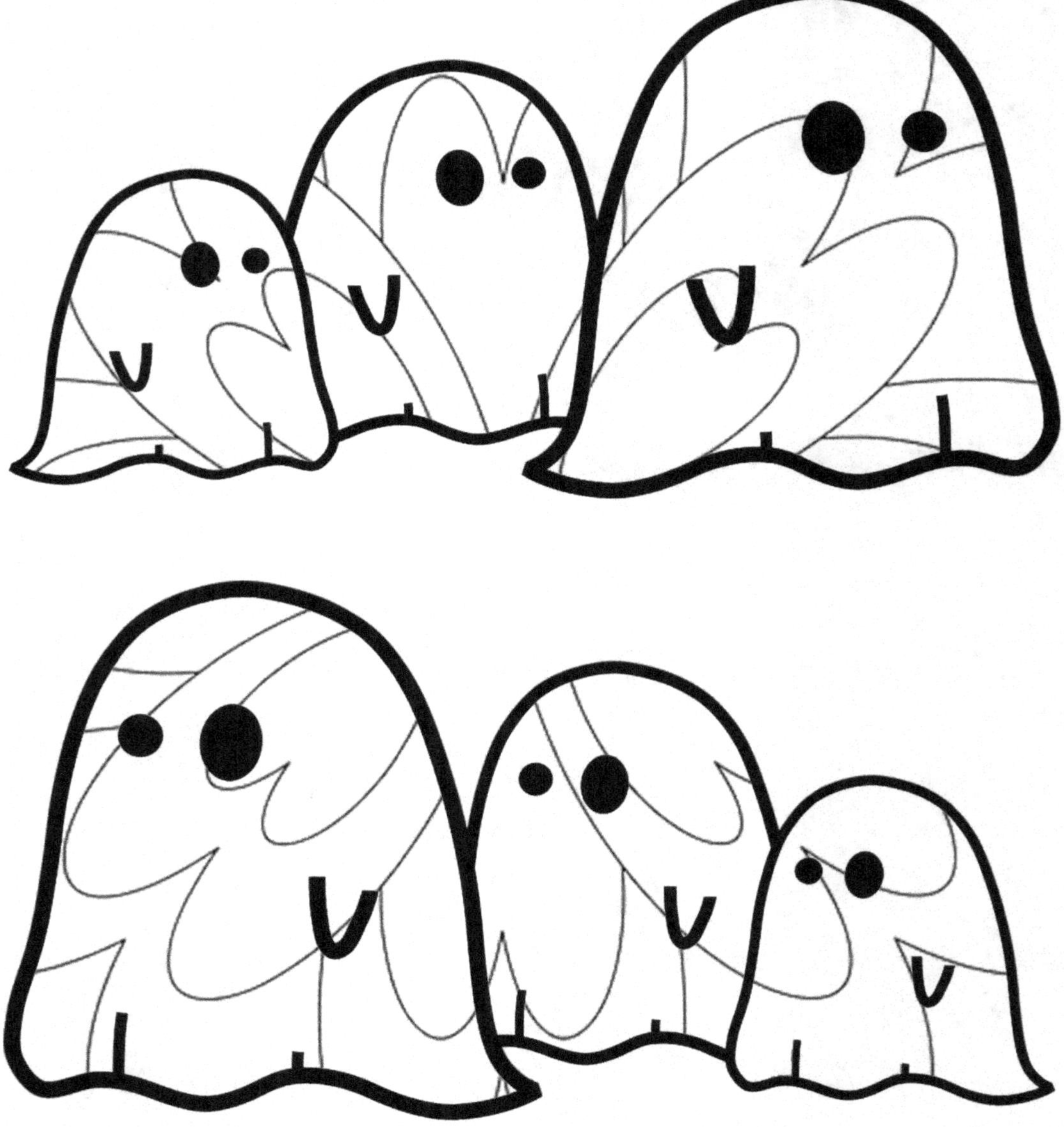

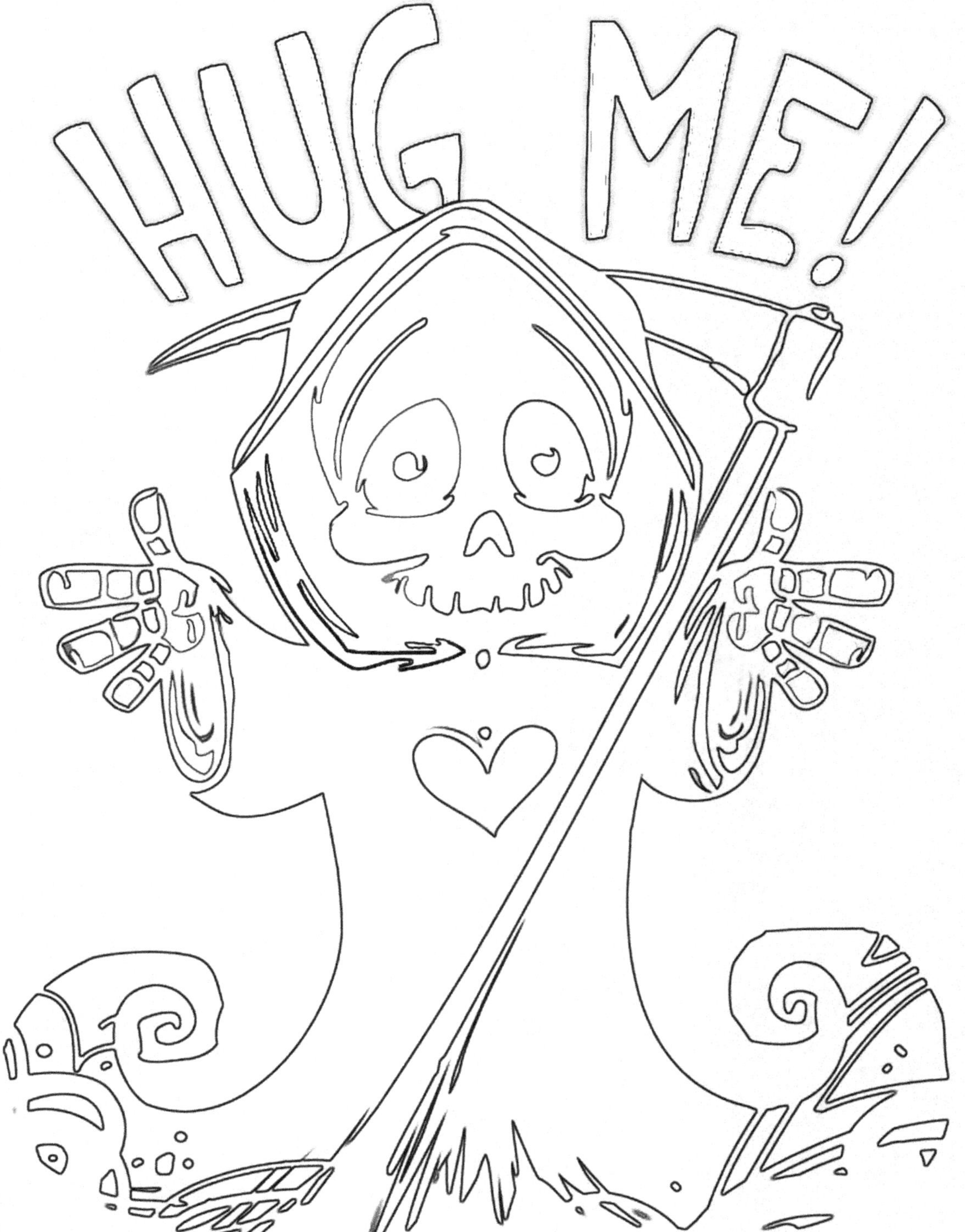
HUG ME!

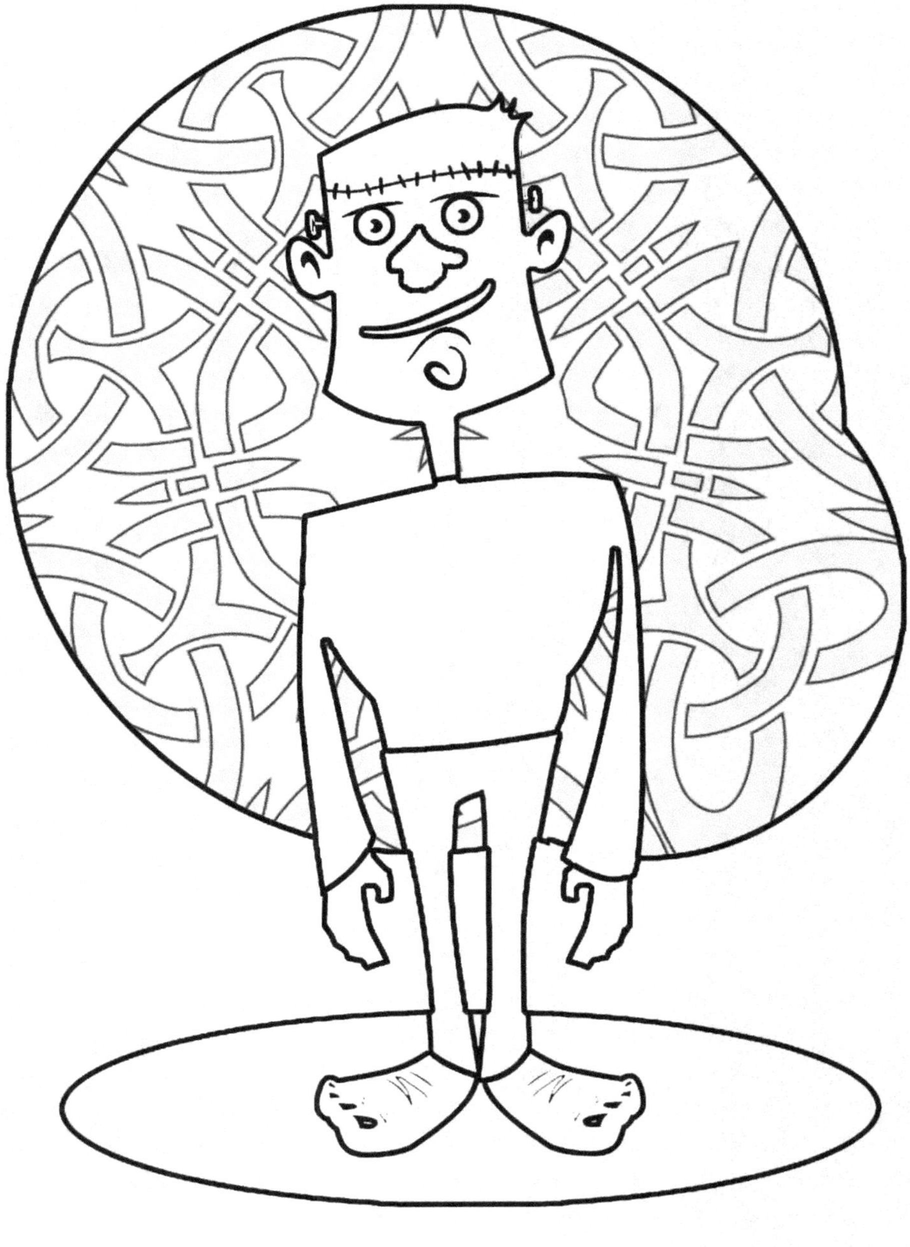

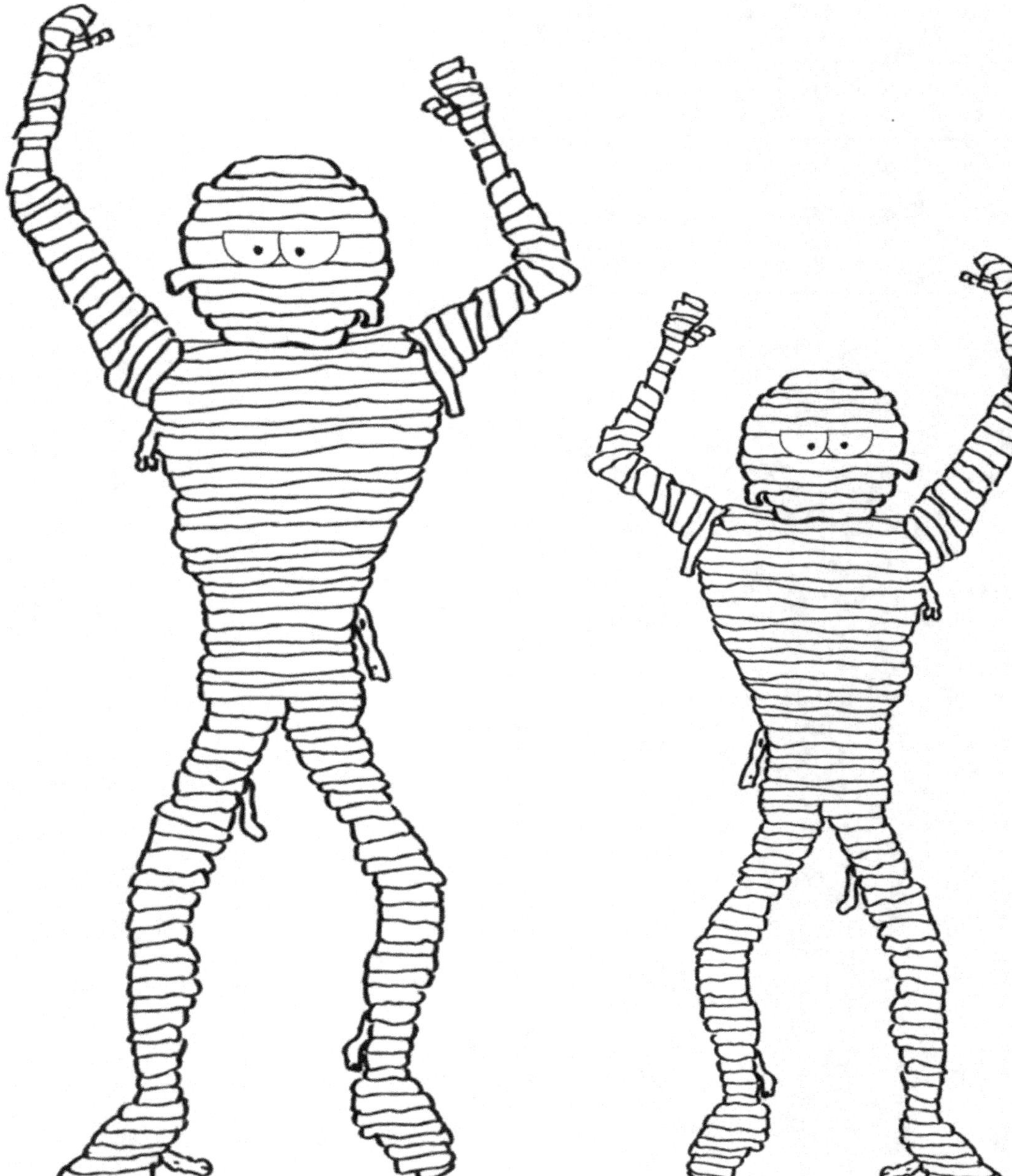

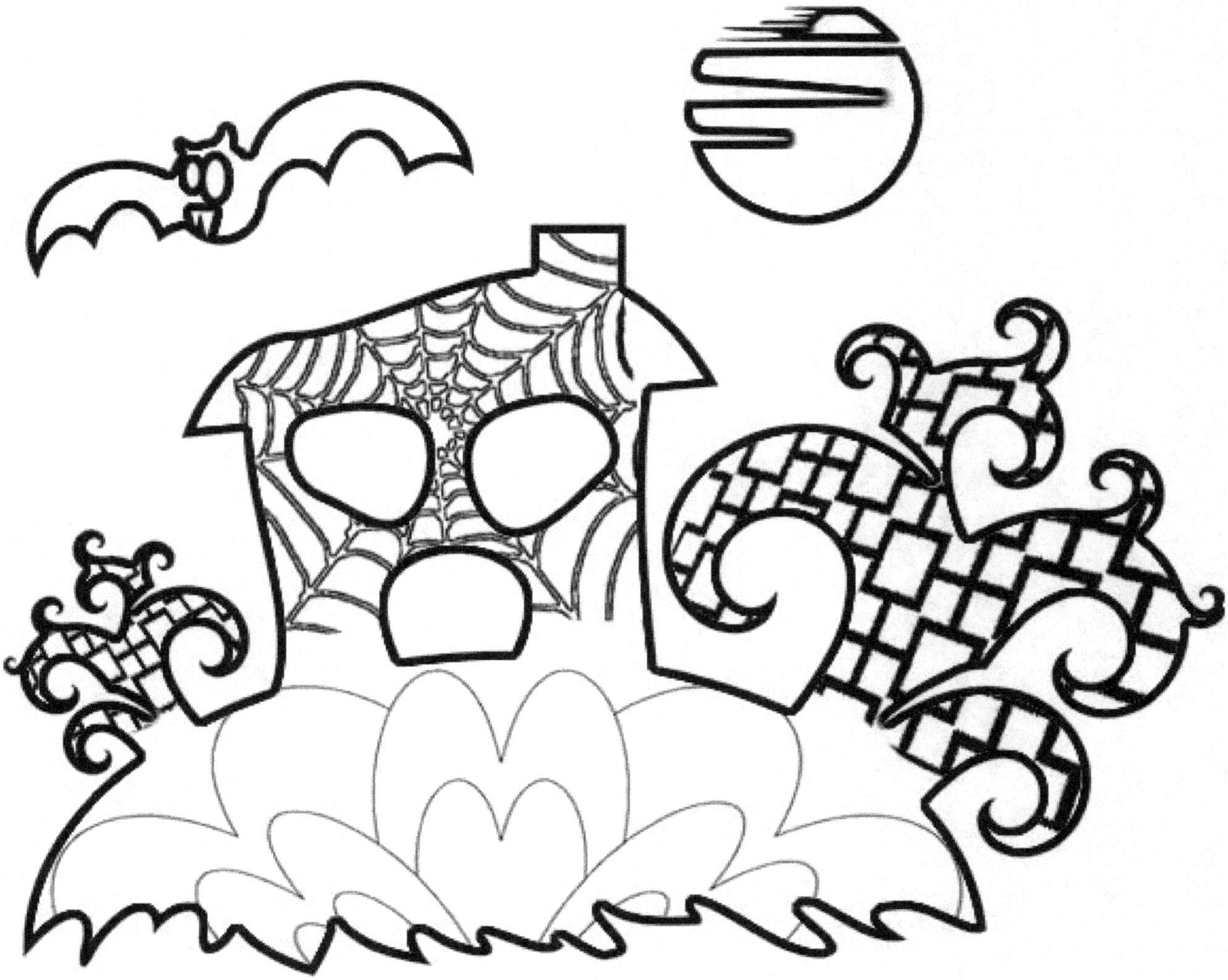

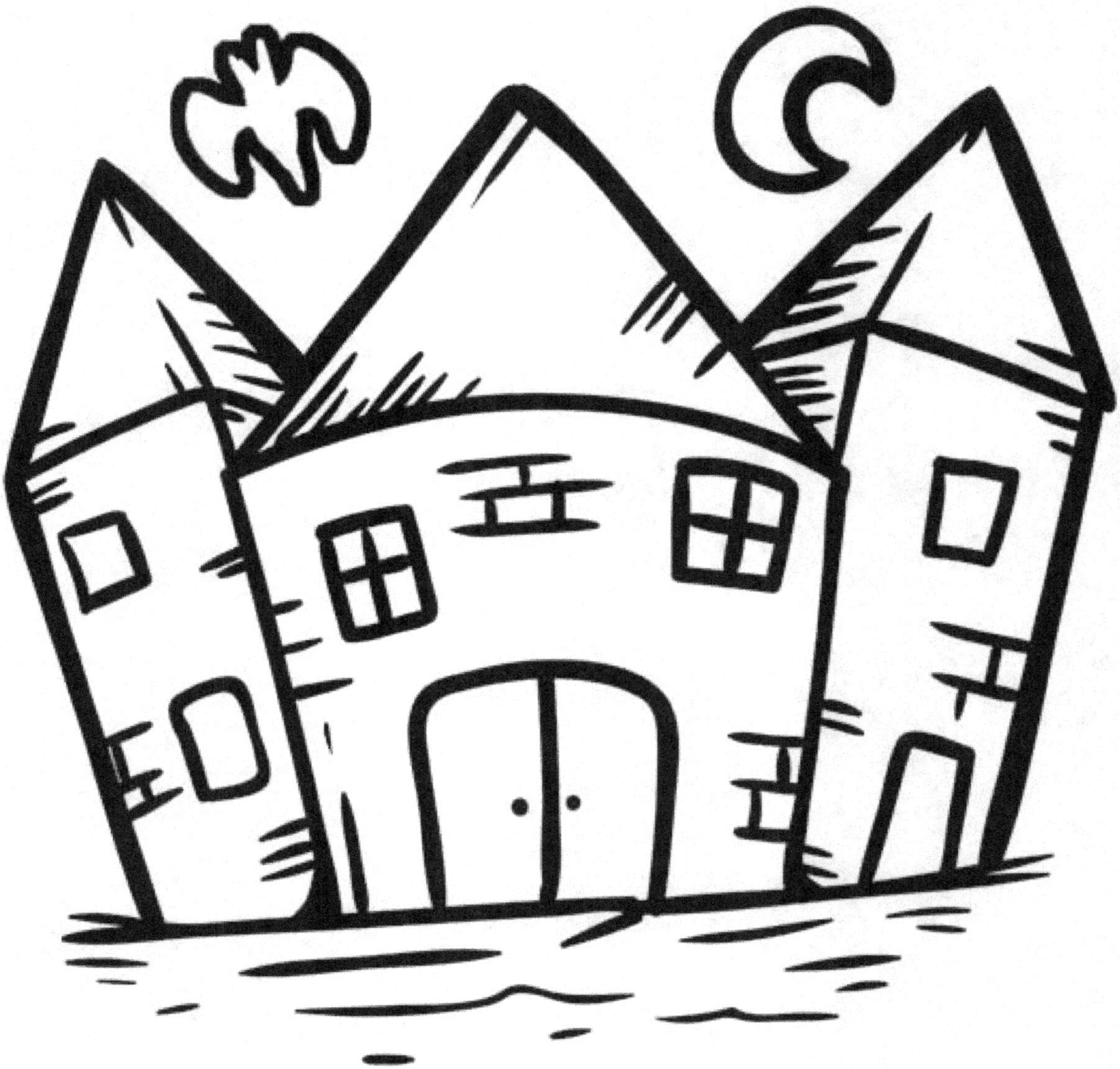

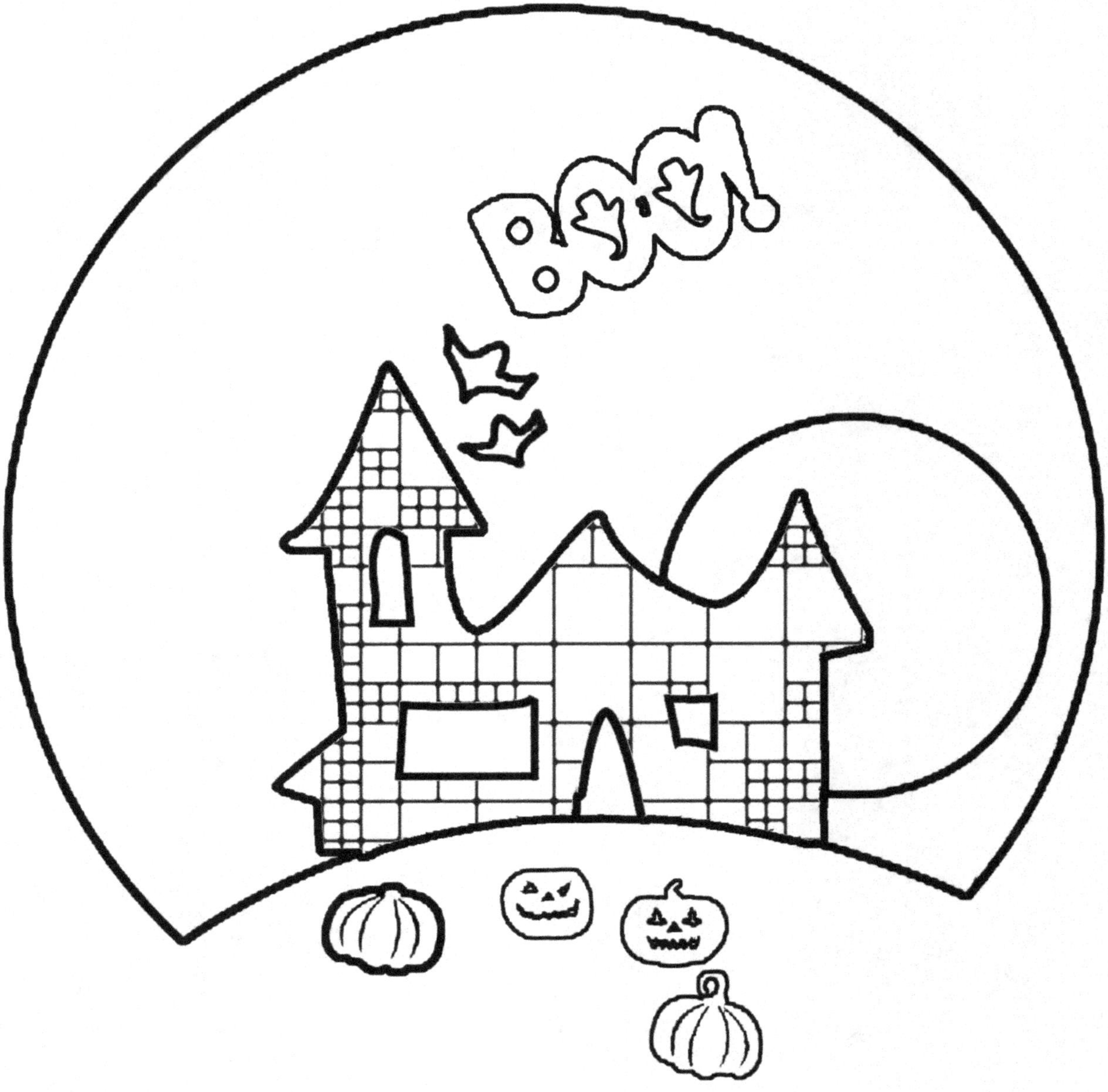
BOO!

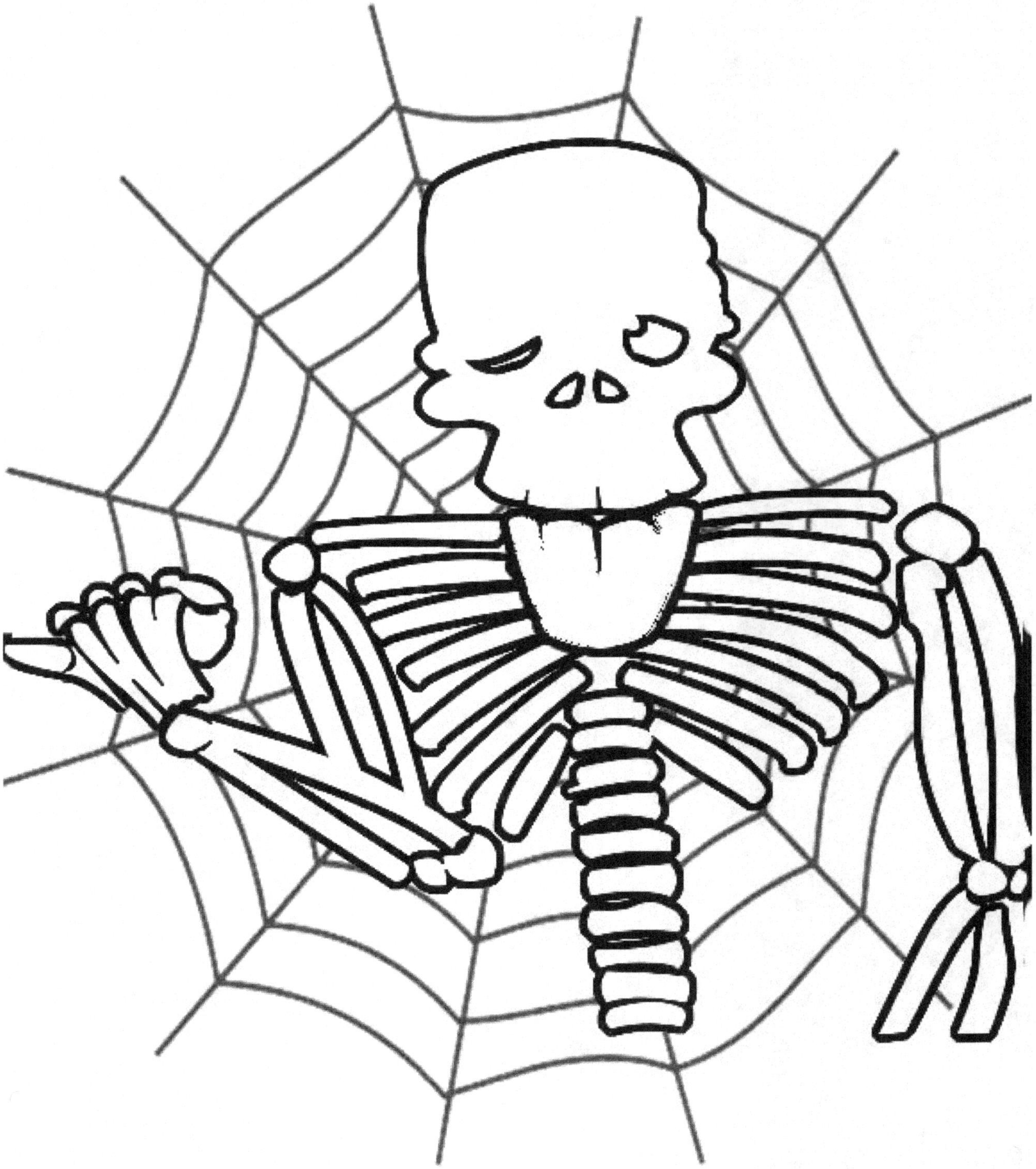

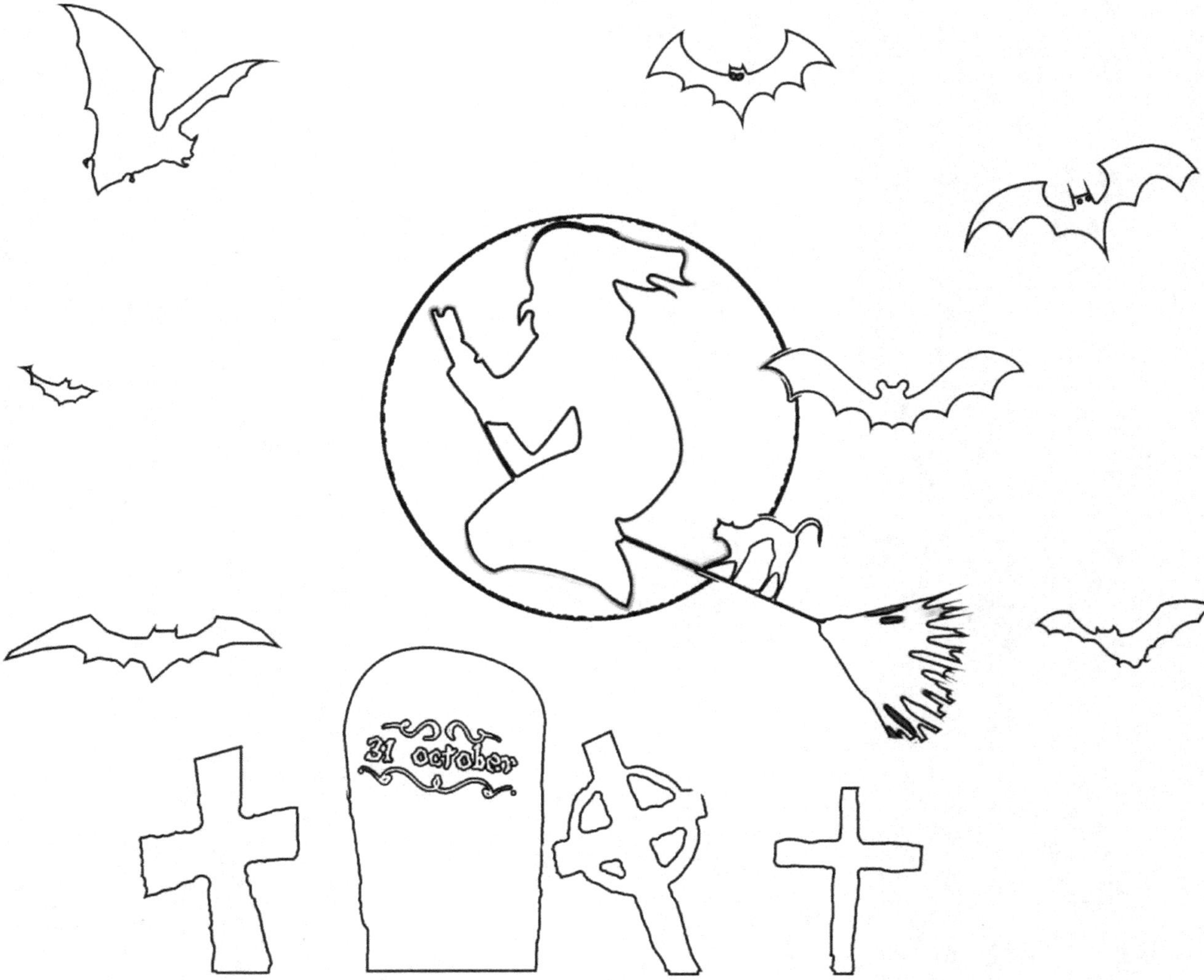
31 october

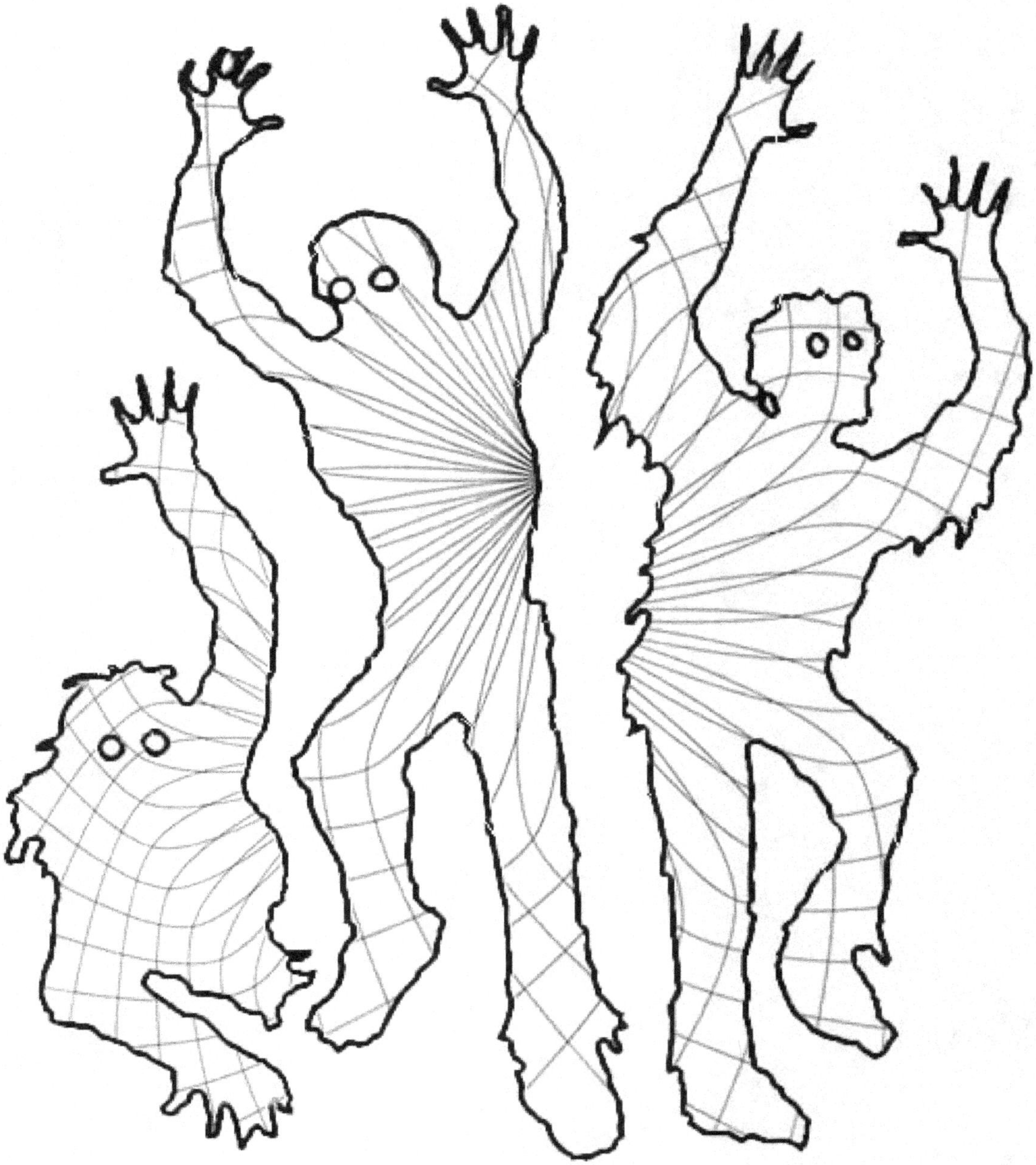

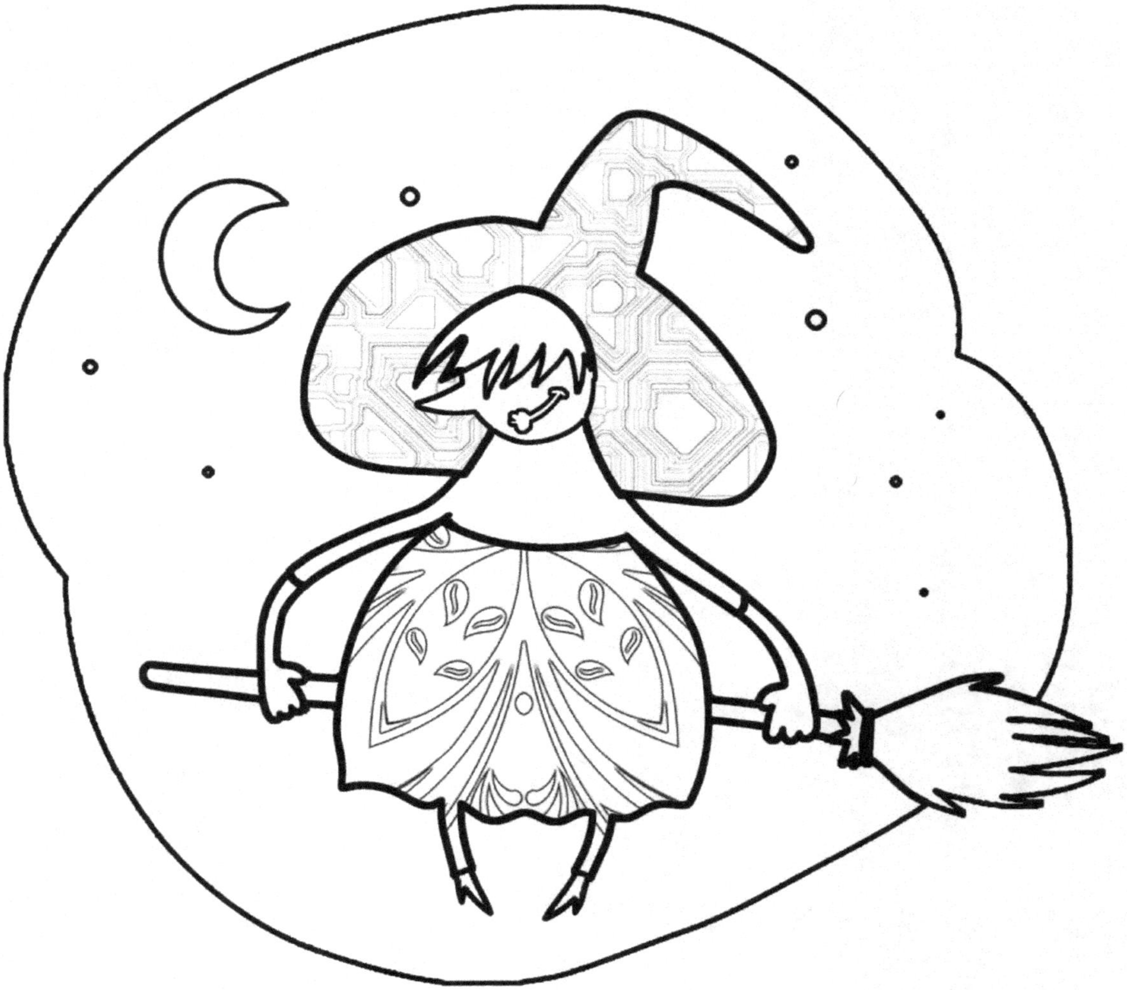

Trick or Treat

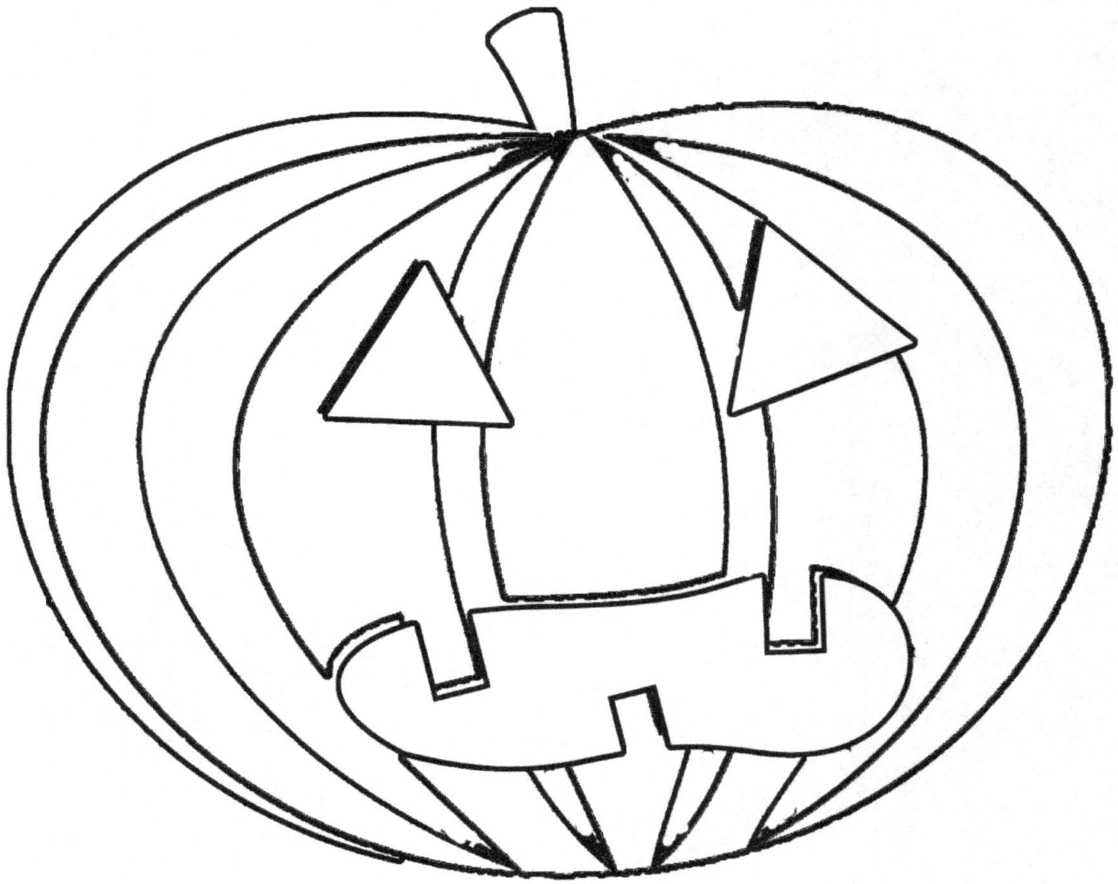

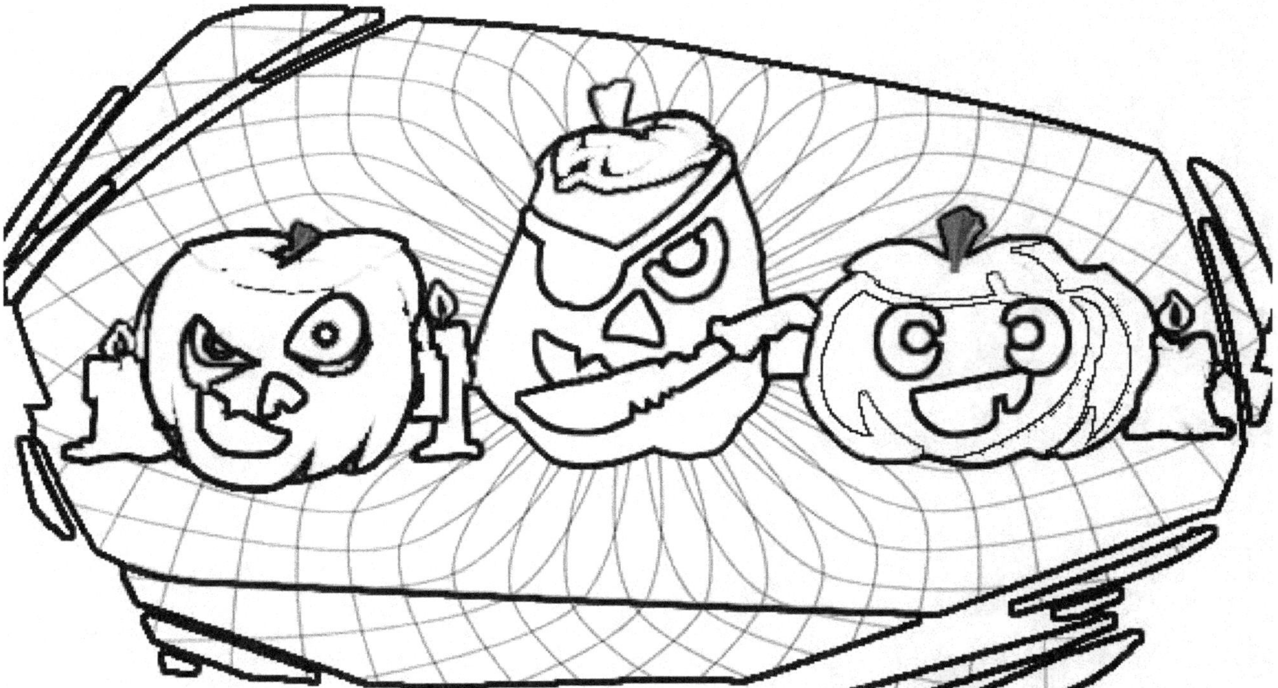

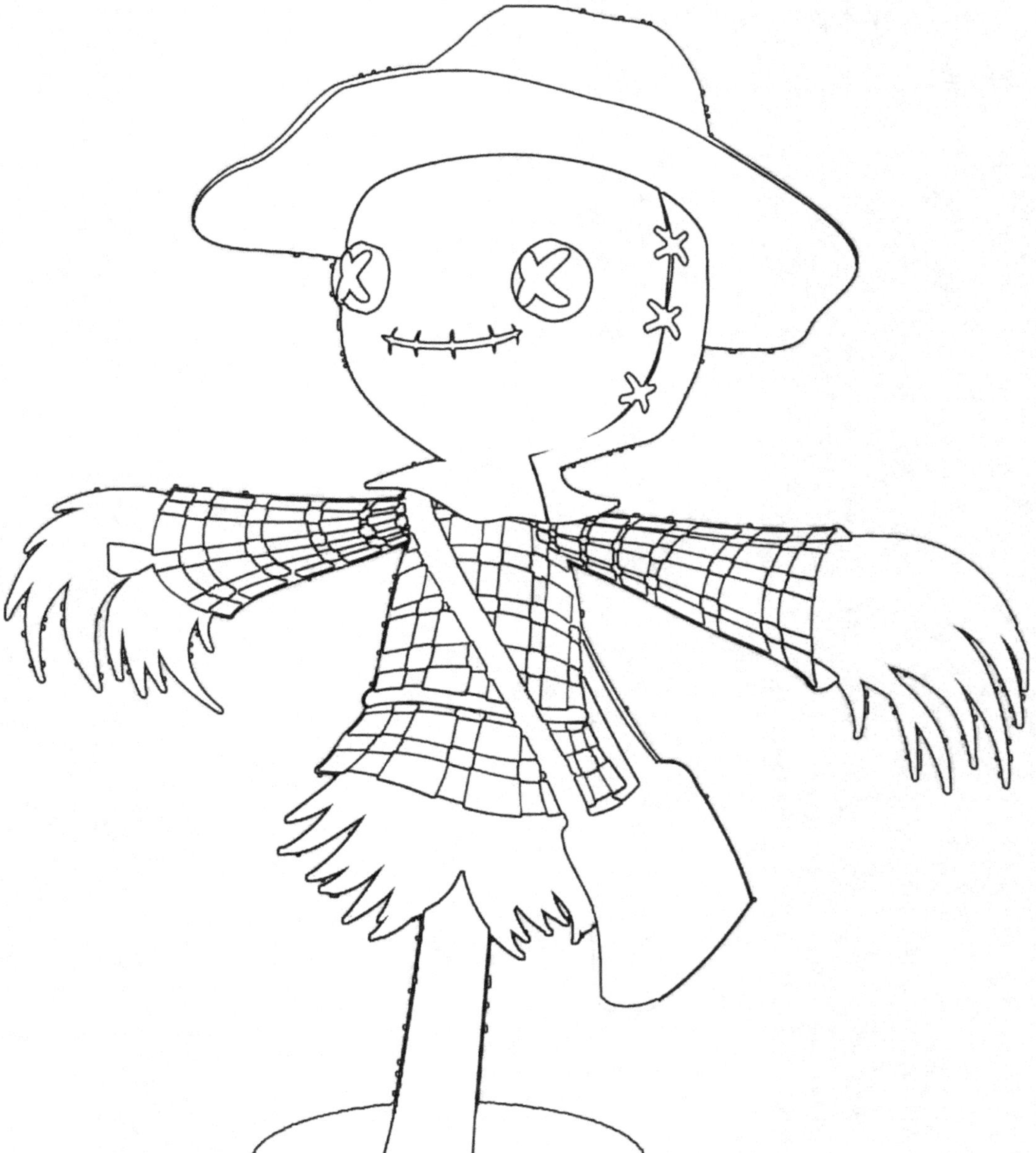

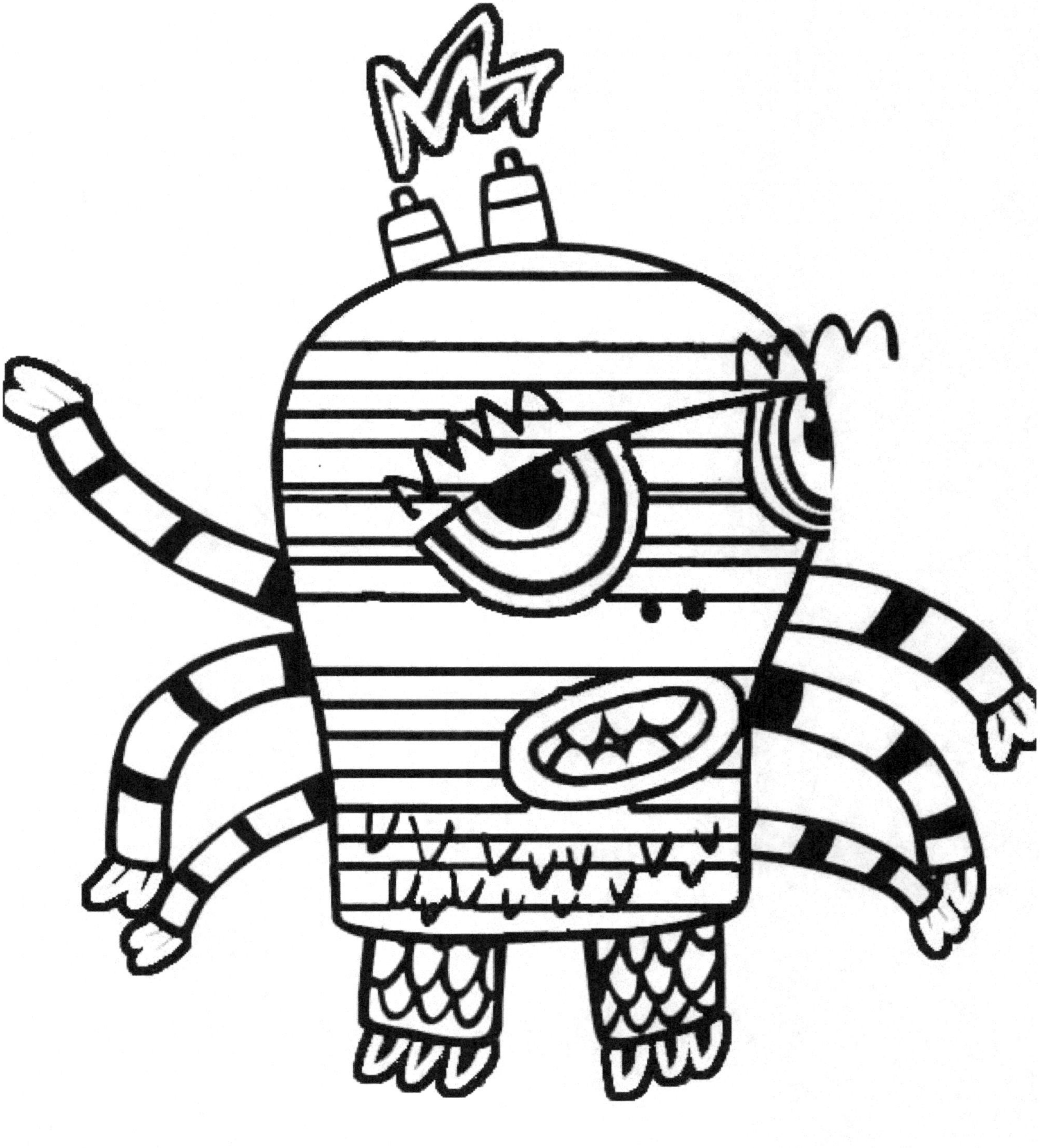

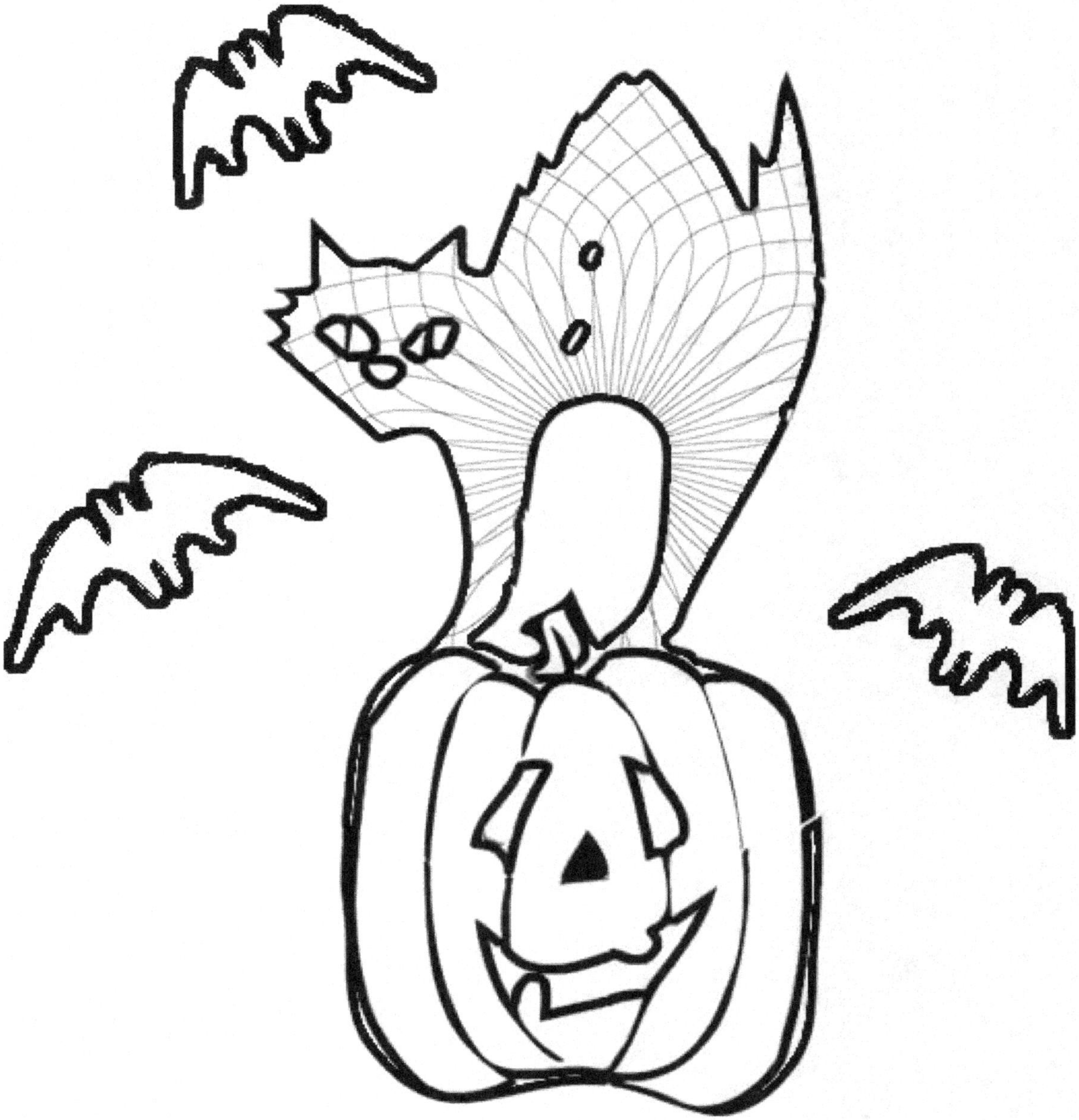

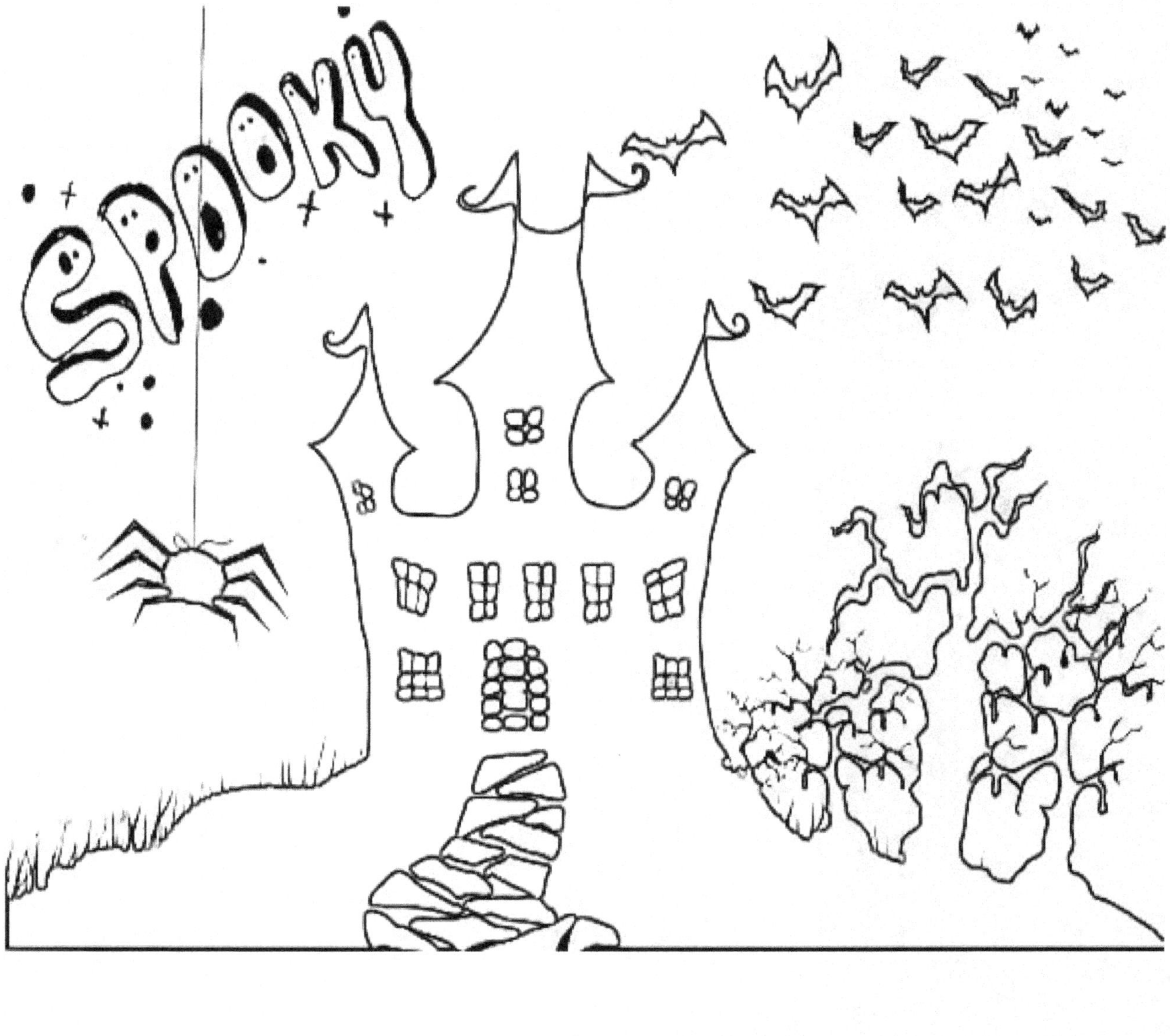
SPOOKY

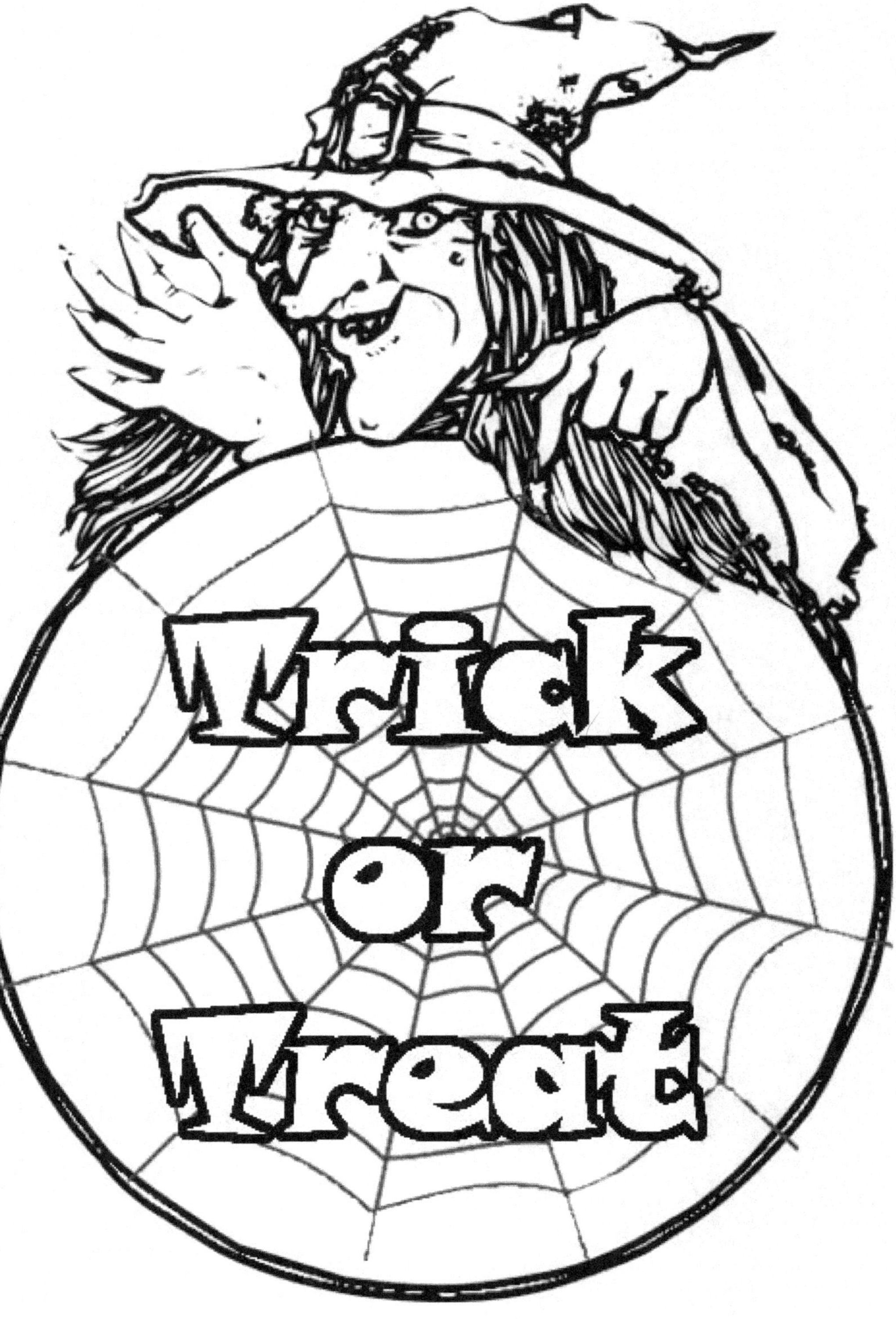
Trick
or
Treat

Thank you

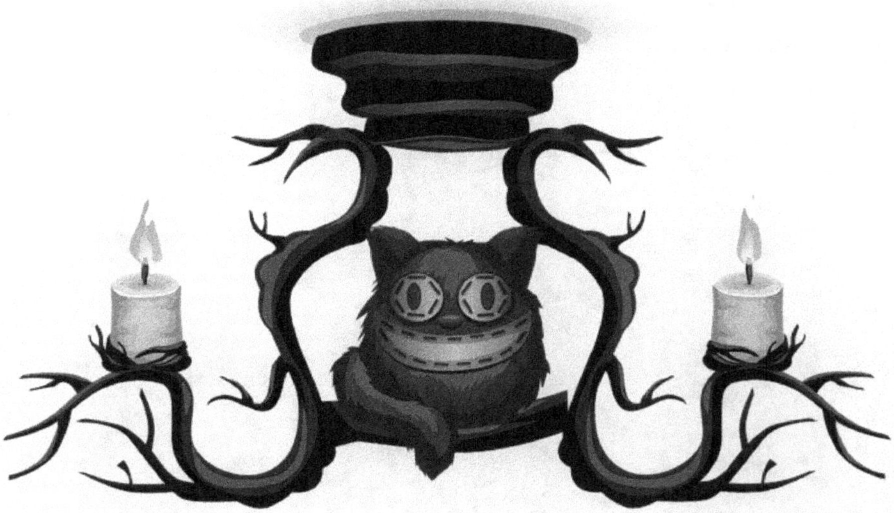

www.ingramcontent.com/pod-product-compliance
Lightning Source LLC
Chambersburg PA
CBHW081125180526
45170CB00008B/3015
* 9 7 8 1 5 3 9 8 1 5 4 4 0 *